GoPro Hero 12

A Concise User Guide to Master GoPro Hero 12
Black For Beginners

Praixel Fadal

Contents

INTRODUCTION

In an era where memories are meant to be lived and shared in high definition, the GoPro Hero 12 camera emerges as a trailblazer, offering an unparalleled avenue to capture and immortalize your adventures.

Whether you're soaring down mountain trails, surfing epic waves, or simply living life to the fullest, the Hero 12 is your steadfast companion in documenting every heartbeat of the action.

We invite you to embark on a journey that will elevate your storytelling capabilities to new heights. Whether you're a seasoned videographer or a novice explorer, this book caters to all levels of expertise, offering insights, techniques, and tricks that will transform your footage into captivating narratives.

What Awaits You:

- **Unveiling the Hero 12:** Get acquainted with the Hero 12's features, capabilities, and accessories that enable you to capture dynamic content in any environment.

- **Capturing Cinematic Shots:** Dive into the world of composition, framing, and storytelling techniques that will bring your footage to life.

- **Navigating the Interface:** Whether you're adjusting settings or accessing modes, we guide you through the camera's interface to ensure seamless operation.

- **Optimizing Settings:** From resolution to frame rates, discover the optimal settings for various scenarios, ensuring your footage is of the highest quality.

- **Harnessing Advanced Modes:** Learn how to use advanced features such as HyperSmooth, Time-Warp, and SuperPhoto to add flair and drama to your shots.

- **Editing Your Footage:** Explore post-production techniques that will transform raw footage into polished masterpieces, complete with transitions, effects, and soundtracks.

- **Sharing Your Adventures:** From social media platforms to creating immersive VR experiences, uncover avenues to share your stories with the world.

This book is not just about using a camera; it's about embracing a lifestyle of adventure and storytelling. Through its pages, you'll gain the skills to capture heart-pounding moments, curate breathtaking narratives, and preserve memories that will last a lifetime.

CHAPTER ONE: Features of GoPro Hero 12

Video and image capturing are improving daily, and so is the technology being used. GoPro remains one of the best for cameras, and the newest additions to their lineup prove it in every sense. It is packed full of different unique features.

Announced in September 2022, the GoPro Hero 12 is the successor to the GoPro Hero 10, which was a game changer in many ways. Though this newest edition has several similarities to its successor, it also has several updated features.

In this chapter, you will learn about the new features of GoPro Hero 12, ranging from its new and advanced sensor to water-resistant, improved battery capacity and video editing tools. Here are the new features of the new GoPro Hero 12:

Designs:

At a glance, the GoPro Hero 12 looks almost exactly like its predecessor, except for the blue numbering on the side. They are the same size and weight and have the same design, right down to the power button and battery placement. Even though there are a lot of similarities, here are some noticeable new features;

- **Waterproof:** The GoPro Hero 12 is entirely waterproof and can survive up to 10 meters of water.

- **Improved Sensor Design:** Internally though, there are a few changes. Most notable is the larger 27MP 1/1.9" sensor. This allows it to shoot in an

8:7 aspect ratio that is perfect for vertical videos. This is consistent with GoPro's gradual shift from purely an action camera to a camera for content creation as well.

- **Full frame:** this tool allows you to shoot 8:7 5.3k video. This video can later be reframed in different aspect ratios. Thus from the same video, you can get clips optimized for traditional landscape video, like YouTube. And also get vertical videos for popular video-sharing platforms like tiktok.

- **360 Horizontal Lock:** This feature allows the software AI to note the horizon and maintain an upright orientation even as the camera moves through a 360-degree rotation. This feature is available at most resolutions except 5.3K@60fps, 4K@120fps, 2.7K@240fps , and 1080p@240fps, at which horizontal lock is limited to 27 degrees.

Battery Capacity:

Here are some of the new features as regarding the battery capacity in the GoPro Hero 12;

- **Enduro Battery:** The GoPro Hero 12 is powered by a removable, rechargeable, 1,720mAh lithium-ion Enduro battery. This was first introduced with the GoPro Hero 10. Unlike the GoPro Hero 10, the battery is now sold with the camera.

- **Improved Battery Life:** The battery now gives up to 40% more battery life than its predecessor. The exact battery life varies with activity - WiFi, GPS, and higher resolutions drain the battery faster. Generally, the battery lasts anywhere between an hour and a half to two hours.

- **Extended Battery Mode:** You can increase use time even more by shooting in the Extended Battery Mode.

- **Fast Charging:** Charging the battery is quite fast too. The Enduro battery can get a full charge in two to three hours with a wired charger.

Camera Specs:

The GoPro Hero 12 is an upgrade over its predecessor in many ways. Here are some of the notable changes:

- **Smart Color:** One notable new feature is the 10-bit color. This allows GoPro to shoot videos and stills with colors that are more true to life and less oversaturated.

- **Increased Aspect Ratio:** In addition to the new 8:7 aspect ratio that the larger sensor affords, you can also shoot in more traditional formats like 16:9 and 4:3.

- **Wider Angle:** You can now get an even wider angle shot than ever before on the GoPro Hero 12. This is due to the new Hyperview mode.

- **Capturing Options:** You also get more options for capturing still shots with the GoPro Hero 12. You can now extract beautiful 24.7MP stills from videos. This way, you can take advantage of every moment.

- **Easy mode:** With easy mode, you can stay aware of the multiple options of what to do and how to do them when taking videos.

- **Pro mode:** This mode allows you more freedom to fine-tune every little detail before taking your shot.

- **Burst Mode:** With Burst mode, you can now capture RAW images rather than just JPEG.

Video Stabilization:

The GoPro Hero 12 comes with HyperSmooth v5.0 , which comes with even better video stabilization. HyperSmooth 5.0 also comes with other built-in features like

- **AutoBoost:** this automatically determines how much stabilization your video needs, so you don't have to be making adjustments to get that smooth, shake-free effect.

- **Horizon Lock:** This notes the horizon level and keeps your video perfectly oriented even when the camera rotates. This feature is newly incorporated into HyperSmooth.

Another new feature of HyperSmooth on the GoPro Hero 12 is that it needs to crop in more closely due to the larger sensor. This is quite noticeable when using this video stabilization feature.

Video Recording Capability:

With video stabilization and a host of features and modes, the GoPro Hero 12 shoots like a dream. Regarding resolution, video capacity is almost the same - 5.3K video at up to 60 fps, 4K video at up to 120 fps, and 2.7K at up to 240 fps.

10-bit color means that your videos appear more true to life. The videos have good dynamic range and little noise. However, low-light situations are still a challenge for the GoPro Hero 12.

Another feature worth noting is the Auto Highlight feature. If you have a Quik subscription, your videos automatically upload when you plug in your GoPro Hero 12 to charge.

These short highlight videos are clipped out, showing the best parts of your captured footage. These short highlights can be uploaded immediately to any platform of your choice.

The GoPro Hero 12 also comes with three new time-lapse preset modes for low-light photography. These create a shorter presentation of an event that occurs over a longer period. The presets are:

- **Star Trails:** these create beautiful trails across the sky to mark the movements of the stars as the earth rotates.

- **Vehicle Light Trails:** these create exciting patterns from vehicle lights. This mode comes with the option to choose trail length - short, long, or maximum.

- **Light Painting:** capture beautiful patterns in this mode using a handheld light source. You can create different types of patterns with this.

Storage Capacity:

Although the GoPro Hero 12 ships with a 32GB microSD card, it can take a microSD card of up to 512GB. However, not all cards can work with the GoPro Hero 12. The limiting factor is speed. To know which card to get for your GoPro Hero 12, here are a few guidelines:

- Type: MicroSD Card

- Rating: V30 or UHS-3

- Storage Capacity: 32/64/128/256/512GB

A GoPro subscription will also get you unlimited cloud storage and automatic uploads. Another reason to get a subscription is that you also get impressive discounts on the GoPro Hero 12 and its accessories.

Accessories:

The GoPro Hero 12 comes with only a few bits and ends in the box:

1. A short USB-A to USB-C type cord for charging and data transfer

2. An adhesive mouth for sticking your GoPro Hero 12 to flat surfaces

3. A buckle mouth that fits into the foldable fingers at the bottom of the GoPro Hero 12 and helps to attach it to other accessories

4. A thumb screw

5. A single Enduro battery

6. Decorative stickers.

Other than these, there are whole lists of different accessories compatible with the GoPro Hero 12.

CHAPTER TWO: Understanding the Basics

The GoPro Hero 12 Black is a game changer regarding camera coverage with unimaginable image quality. The camera has all you need, with several mounting options and unlimited cloud backup. In this chapter, you will learn the basics of Hero 12 Black and how to get started.

Component of GoPro Hero 12

The way the GoPro Hero 12 is made is very similar to that of the last two models. Here are the different components of the GoPro Hero 12;

1. At the top is the **"Shutter Button."** This is for taking pictures and starting/stopping video recording.

2. Next to the shutter button at the top is a **"Microphone."**

3. The **"Power Button"** is on the camera's right side, and right above it is the number 12 printed in blue.

4. On the left side, there are no buttons.

5. At the front is the **"Lens."** It is covered with a detachable lens cover. The glass of the lens cover is covered with a thin oleophobic coating to repel water.

6. Also at the front is the smaller 1.4" display.

7. The back features a larger 2.27" touchscreen display.

How to Charge the Battery of GoPro Hero 12

With only about an hour or two of battery life per Enduro battery, you will often need to keep your battery charged. This is not a challenge, as the GoPro Hero 12 design is similar to the past two models. This means that there is a USB-C port above the battery. Here is how to charge the Hero 12;

- Open the battery cover slip by sliding the tab at the bottom down and pulling the slip.

- With the battery in, plug a USB-C cord into the port. Then connect the other end to a light source.

- If the battery is properly connected and charging, a red light appears on both the front and rear displays. Once the battery is fully charged, the light will go off.

TIPS: *Here are some tips to note after purchasing the GoPro Hero camera;*

- *The GoPro Hero 12 does come with a USB-C to USB-A cord for charging. However, you can use any USB-C cable - even your phone charger.*

- *If you have multiple batteries, you can get an adapter plug. With this, you slip the battery in and connect it to a light source. There are various types of adapters, and some can even charge multiple batteries at a time.*

NOTE: *If this light doesn't come on when you plug your GoPro Hero 12, pull the battery out a little, then push it back in.*

Power ON/OFF GoPro Hero 12

After unboxing your device, as recommended, the next step is to charge your camera's battery until it gets to 100% battery life. You first have to turn it on to get started with the GoPro Hero 12. This is really easy, and here is how to go about it;

- Press the power button on the side down till the camera gives some little beeps and the displays turn on.

- While turning the GoPro Hero 12 off, Press and hold the power button, and the camera will give a couple of tiny beeps before powering down.

Initial Setup of GoPro Hero 12

Before you can start using your new GoPro Hero 12, you have to set it up. Before you start, make sure to charge the battery.

- First, "**Power ON**" the GoPro Hero 12.

- Select your "**Language**," then click the check mark.

- Next is to agree to legal terms and conditions. Ensure to select the "**Agree**" button to GoPro's terms and conditions.

- **GPS** - choose whether you want it on or off. Having your GPS turned on allows geo-tagging of pictures and videos.

- Now, you have to connect your camera to the Quik app. You can update your camera software and transfer files to the Quik app cloud storage.

- Open the Quik app on your smartphone.

- Click the GoPro option at the bottom of the screen.

- Click the add icon at the upper left to add your new camera.

- The app will automatically scan and detect your GoPro Hero 12.

- Click on *Connect to the camera* to initiate pairing.

- Next, you can change your camera name as it appears on your Quik app. By default, it should be *Hero 12 Black.*

- Next, update the camera's software. You might have to agree to GoPro's terms and conditions again. This might take a couple of minutes.

How to Insert Memory Card

You'll need a memory card to save the pictures and footage you take with your GoPro Hero 12. The GoPro Hero 12 can take up to a 512GB microSD card. To insert the memory card;

- Open the battery cover slip by sliding the tab at the bottom down and pulling the slip.

- Insert the card into the memory card slot with the front facing the back of the camera.

- Press down the memory card until it clicks into place.

- After carrying out all these steps, your memory card is ready for use.

How to Format Memory Card

Formatting your memory card will wipe or clean, or delete all your photos, videos, and any other data saved on the memory card. You can format the memory card for your GoPro Hero 12 while it is still inserted. To do this;

- On the rear display, slide your finger down from the top of the screen to **"Open the Quick Menu."**

- Swipe sideways to view other options, then select **"Preferences."**

- Scroll down the page of options till you find **"Reset,"** and click on it.

- Next, select **"Format SD card,"** then click **"Format"** again to complete the process.

Basic Tips of GoPro Hero 12

Here are some basic info and tips about the GoPro Hero 12 that will be of help to beginners;

How to turn GoPro that won't turn ON

What can you do if your GoPro Hero 12 fails to turn on for some reason? Here are a few things you can try these steps;

- First, unplug the camera and remove the battery and SD card. Reinsert the battery after a brief period and try to turn it on. If the camera doesn't respond, wait a few seconds and try again.

- Connect the camera without a battery to a direct wall charger rated at least 5V/1A. Use the USB-C cable that came with the GoPro Hero 12. Watch for any flashing lights, and try to turn it on again after a few seconds.

- Try again using different cables or charging sources. If the camera turns on, disconnect the cable, and reconnect it after reinserting the battery. Try to turn it on again; if this fails, contact GoPro support.

- After reconnecting with the battery inserted, the red indicator should come on. However, this may take some time if the battery is very low.

- After charging for a while, disconnect the camera and try to turn it on. If it still doesn't come on, contact GoPro support.

How much time does the GoPro take to charge completely:

The time required to get a full charge on the GoPro Hero 12 Enduro battery depends on the charging source. If charging directly from an optimally rated wall charger, you can get a full charge in as little as two hours.

If charging indirectly from another device, like a computer or a portable power storage device, it may require up to four hours to get a full charge. So, charging a GoPro Hero 12 Enduro battery to full capacity takes between two to four hours.

CHAPTER THREE:
GoPro Camera App

The GoPro Hero uses an app known as the Quik app. It is an app that allows you to pick your best shots, sync them to music, add cinematic transitions, and create a shareable video. This chapter will teach you about the Quik app and how to get started.

Download GoPro Quik (Android)

The Quik app grants you access to cloud storage and editing options. With it, you can view, download and edit photos and footage taken with the GoPro Hero 12 right from your mobile device. Here is how to download the Quik app for Android;

- Open the Google play store app.

- In the search bar, type GoPro Quik.

- Find the app from the search results and click install.

- After installing, enable the app, and you're good to go.

NOTE: If you search in the play store and can't find the Quik app, it could be because the latest version is incompatible with your device. Only Android devices with Android 9.0 or newer and at least 2GB RAM can use this latest version.

TIP: You can download an older version from verified sites if your device does not have these specs. Ensure to use malware protection software to safeguard your device.

Download GoPro Quik (iPhone/iPad)

Getting the GoPro Quik app on your iOS or iPadOS device is also very easy.

- Open the Apple play store on your device.

- In the search bar, type GoPro Quik.

- Select the Quik app from the search engine results and click on it.

- Click the *'Get'* button beside the app information, and then click *'Install'*.

- You must be signed in to your apple account to download.

NOTE: Again, you can only download the latest version of the GoPro Quik app unto devices with iOS 14, or iPadOS 14 or newer. You can also find the Quik app faster by simply scanning the QR code in the paperwork that comes with the GoPro Hero 12.

How to Update the GoPro Hero App

What if you already have an older version of the Quik app? If you have automatic updates turned on, your app should update to the latest version with ease. If you want to update the app manually,

- Open play store, or Apple app store on your device.

- In the search bar, type GoPro Quik.

When you find the app, click the 'Update' button beside the app information. This will download the newest version onto your device.

CHAPTER FOUR:
Settings Up GoPro

The possibilities for capturing unforgettable moments are endless when using your GoPro HERO. This powerful camera is capable of recording broadcast-quality video and eye-catching photos, offering a variety of setting options to choose from.

However, setting up your shots correctly is the most important factor when recording these moments. As a new GoPro user, it may be difficult to filter through the options.

In this chapter, we will provide a simplified guide to setting up the GoPro's Hero 12. You will learn how to get started with the GoPro camera.

Meet HERO12 Black:

Here are the different compartment of GoPro Hero 12:

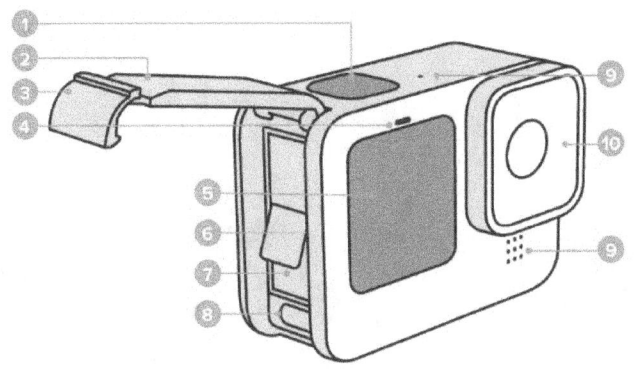

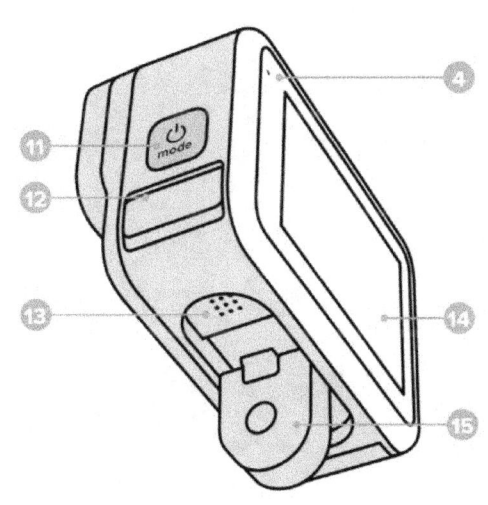

(1) Shutter Button

(2) Door

(3) Door Latch

(4) Status Light

(5) Front Screen

(6) SD Card Slot

(7) Battery

(8) USB-C Port

(9) Microphone

(10) Removable Lens

(12) Mode Button

(12) Drain Port

(13) Speaker

(14) Touch Screen **(15)** Folding Fingers

Setting Up Your Camera:

With a little planning and preparation, you can easily set up your GoPro Hero 12 camera and start capturing amazing footage. Here are the steps on how to set up your GoPro Hero 12 camera:

SD CARDS:

A microSD memory card is essential to ensure optimal storage for your videos and images. It is recommended to choose a reputable brand of memory card that aligns with the following specifications:

Before handling your microSD card, ensure your hands are clean and dry. Additionally, consulting the manufacturer's guidelines is crucial to determining the acceptable temperature range and other vital information related to the usage of your memory card.

Keep in mind that over time, microSD cards may undergo degradation, potentially impacting your camera's ability to store media. If you encounter any issues, replace an older card with a new one.

TIP: To maintain the optimal health of your microSD card, consider periodically reformatting it. Do note that this process will erase all existing media, so ensure you have saved everything beforehand.

- To access the Dashboard, swipe downward on the rear screen.

- For resetting your microSD card, navigate to **Preferences** > **Reset** > **Format SD Card** by swiping left.

SD Card + Battery Setup

- Gently slide the door latch to unlock the GoPro door.

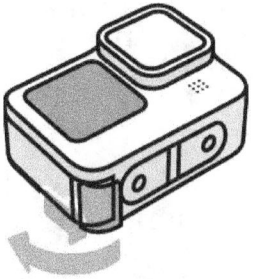

- Slide the SD card into the designated slot; ensure that the label faces the direction of the battery compartment.

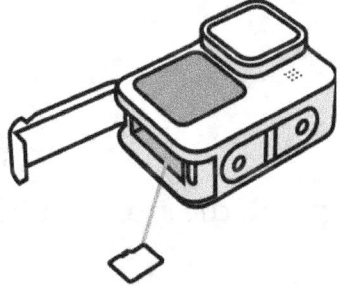

- To remove the card from the slot, gently press it inward using your fingernail until it disengages.

- Insert the battery unit back into its designated compartment.

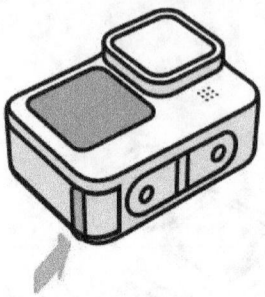

- Connect your camera to a USB charger or computer with the USB-C cable.

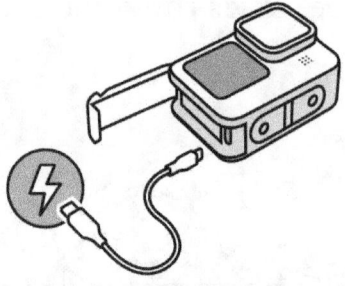

- The camera battery takes about 3 hours to recharge fully, and the indicator light will turn off when it's done.

Tips for Your GoPro:

Update Software: Make sure your HERO12 Black has the latest software for optimal performance. The GoPro Quik app provides the fastest and easiest way to update, but you can also do it manually.

Charge Battery: Your GoPro should come with a partially charged battery, but it's best to fully charge it before use. For optimal performance in cold weather and longer runtime, use only GoPro Enduro batteries with HERO12 Black. Non-GoPro batteries may fit but can limit performance, void warranty, and pose safety risks.

Maximise Battery Life: Maximize your HERO12 Black camera's runtime with Extended Battery mode. Access the Dashboard by swiping down on the rear touch screen, then swipe left and tap Video Mode to enable Extended Battery mode's most energy-efficient resolutions and frame rates.

CHAPTER FIVE:
Getting Started

Congratulations on your new GoPro Hero 12! This camera is a powerful tool that can help you capture amazing footage of your adventures. In this chapter, we will guide you through how to get started using your camera, as well as provide tips and tricks to maximize your GoPro experience.

Whether you are a beginner or an experienced user, this chapter has something for you. We will start by covering the basics of the camera, such as how to power the camera, understand the front screen, and pair the camera with your smartphone.

Power ON the GoPro:

You can power on the GoPro by pressing the Mode button at the side of the camera.

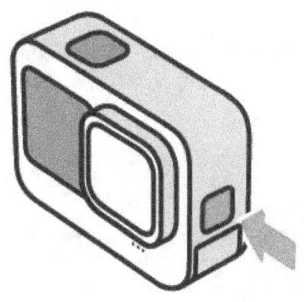

Power OFF the GoPro:

You can power off the GoPro camera by pressing the Mode button for about 3 seconds. Wait patiently, and the camera will turn off.

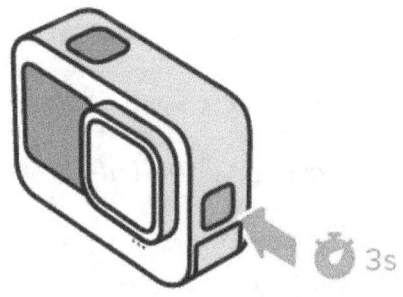

The Front Screen:

The front screen of the GoPro Hero 12 is a small, 1.4-inch LCD display screen that can be used to preview your shots, change settings, and control the camera. Here are some of the things you will notice about the front screen of the GoPro Hero 12:

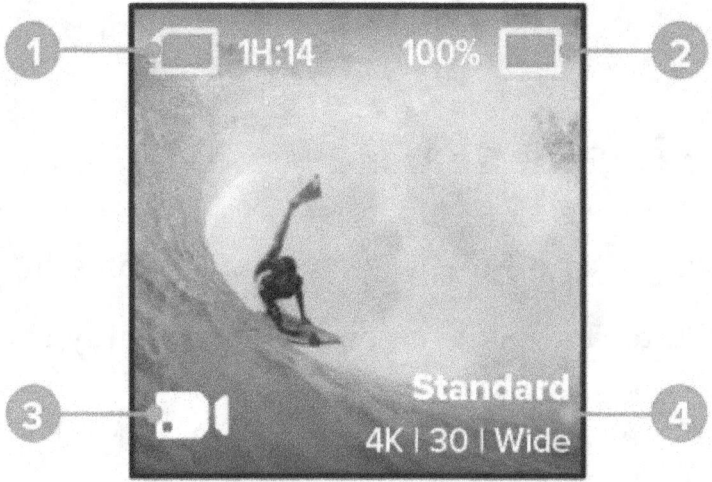

Recording Time/Photos Remaining: The recording time icon is a small clock icon that appears in the top left corner of the screen when the camera is recording. It shows the estimated recording time based on the current settings and the amount of storage space on the microSD card.

Battery Status: The battery status icon is a small, green battery icon located in the rear screen's top right corner. The icon is filled in to indicate the amount of battery life remaining.

A fully filled icon indicates a full battery. As the battery drains, the icon will become less filled in. When the battery is low, the icon will turn red.

Current Mode: The current mode icon is located in the center of the top of the screen. It is a small, circular icon that changes to reflect the camera's current mode (Video, Photo, or Time Lapse).

Capture Settings: The Capture Settings icon is a small gear icon at the bottom of the screen. It is used to access the camera's settings for recording video and taking photos.

Understanding the Touch Screen:

The touch screen of the GoPro Hero 12 is a responsive and user-friendly way to control the camera. Here are the actions that can be carried out with the GoPro camera touch screen:

Tap: You tap on the touch screen to select an item on the display screen.

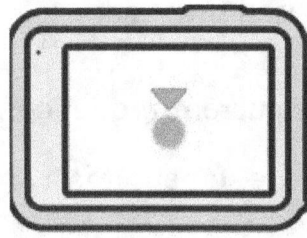

Swipe Left or Right: You can swipe to the left or right to change the camera mode between Video, Photo, and Time Lapse modes.

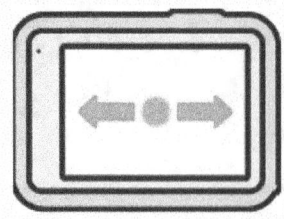

Swipe Down: You can use the swipe-down feature to access the dashboard of your camera in landscape mode.

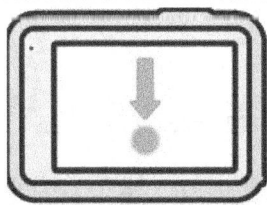

Swipe Up: You can view your most recent photo or video and browse through your Media Gallery by swiping up from the edge of the screen.

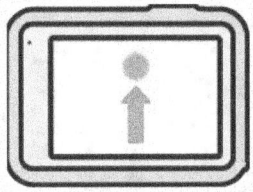

Touch and Hold: You can touch and hold the GoPro screen to reveal the adjust exposure control.

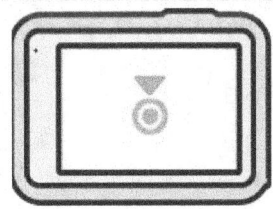

Record Video:

The GoPro Hero 12 uses three capture modes: Video Mode, Photo Mode, and Time Lapse Mode.

To capture or record an event, press the Shutter button at the top of the camera to get started with recording.

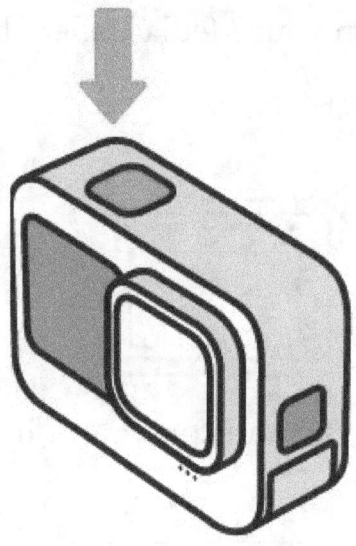

To stop recording your video, press the Shutter button once to save the record.

Snap Photos:

Here are the steps on how to snap photos using the GoPro Hero 12:

- The first step is to turn on the camera.

- Make sure that the camera is in Photo mode. You can do this by swiping left or right on the touch screen until the Photo mode icon is selected.

- Frame your shot and tap the shutter button to take a photo.

CHAPTER SIX: Easy Control

Easy Controls is a feature on the GoPro Hero 12 that simplifies the camera's controls for beginners. With Easy Controls, you can only worry about how much slo-mo you want and which digital lens you want to use.

Easy Controls is a great way to get started with the Go-Pro Hero 12 without worrying about the more advanced settings.

In this chapter, you will learn more about Easy Control. Once you are familiar with the camera, you can always turn off Easy Controls and customize the settings to your liking.

To access Easy Controls, swipe down from the top of the screen and tap on the **"Easy Controls"** icon. You will then see the following options:

Video (Default Mode)

The GoPro easy control mode captures stunning 5.3K resolution video at 30 fps with its versatile Wide digital lens. The camera interface includes onscreen shortcuts to customize the video mode. You will then see two options: Slo-Mo and Digital Lens.

- **Slo-Mo:** This setting determines how much slow motion you want. You can choose from 2x, 4x, 8x, or 10x slow motion.

- **Digital Lens:** This setting determines the field of view of the camera. You can choose from Wide, Linear, Narrow, or SuperView.

Photo:

The GoPro 12 easy control mode allows for snapping breathtaking 27-megapixel images in the unique 8:7 aspect ratio. The photo mode interface, using easy control, offers onscreen shortcuts for lens swapping and timer configuration, streamlining your photographic experience.

Time Lapse:

Delve into time lapses confidently with easy control mode. The GoPro camera captures mesmerizing 4K TimeWarp visuals with a Wide digital lens. A simplified interface offers onscreen shortcuts for swift lens changes and implements a Speed Ramp to elevate dynamism.

Photo using Easy Control

Here are the steps on how to customize Photo Mode using Easy Control in the GoPro Hero 12:

- Turn on the camera and make sure that the camera is in Photo mode. You can do this by swiping left or right on the touch screen until the Photo mode icon is selected.

- Swipe down from the top of the screen to open the Quick Settings menu and select on the **"Easy Controls"** icon.

- Tap on the **"Settings"** icon in the top right corner of the screen and you can now customize the following settings:

1. **Photo resolution:** This setting determines the number of pixels recorded in each photo. Higher resolutions will produce better-quality photos but also take up more storage space.

2. **Photo format:** This setting determines the file format of the photos. You can choose from JPEG or RAW. RAW files give you more flexibility when editing your photos but take up more storage space.

3. **Burst mode:** This setting determines how many photos are taken in quick succession. Higher burst rates will capture more photos, but they will also take up more storage space.

4. **Night Photo:** This mode is designed for taking photos in low light conditions.

5. **SuperPhoto:** This mode uses AI to improve the quality of your photos.

- Once you have finished customizing the settings, tap on the "X" in the top right corner of the screen to close the Settings menu.

Easy Control Tips:

Here are some tips on how to use Easy Control in GoPro Hero 12:

- **Start with Easy Controls:** If you are new to the GoPro Hero 12, use Easy Controls so you can focus on capturing great photos and videos without worrying about technical settings.

- **Experiment with different settings:** Once you become familiar with Easy Controls, you can begin to experiment with various settings. This will aid in your understanding of the camera and how to achieve optimal results.

- **Use the Quick Settings menu:** The Quick Settings menu allows quick access to important settings. To open it, swipe down from the top of the screen.

When to use Easy Control:

- When taking action shots, use Easy Controls for quick photo and video capture.

- Use Easy Controls when you are not sure what settings to use.

- Use Easy Controls when you are sharing your photos and videos with people who are not familiar with photography or videography.

Easy Controls is a great starting point for GoPro Hero 12. It provides access to important settings, but customization requires turning it off.

How to Switch From Easy Control to Pro Control:

Suppose you want more control over your footage. Easy Controls gives you a limited number of settings, while Pro Controls gives you access to all of the camera's settings.

Pro Controls allows you to create custom presets for different shooting conditions. This can save you time when you're setting up your camera. Here is how to switch from easy control to pro control

- The first step is to swipe down from the top to reveal the Dashboard.

- The next step is to swipe from the left of the screen to reveal more options.

- Then tap the control option, and you will be taken to the control interface, where you can change the control.

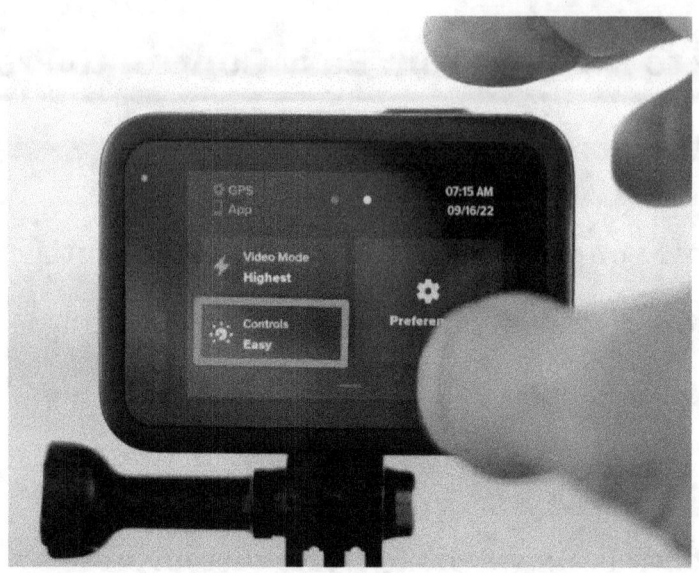

- You can toggle between the Easy and Pro Controls in the control interface.

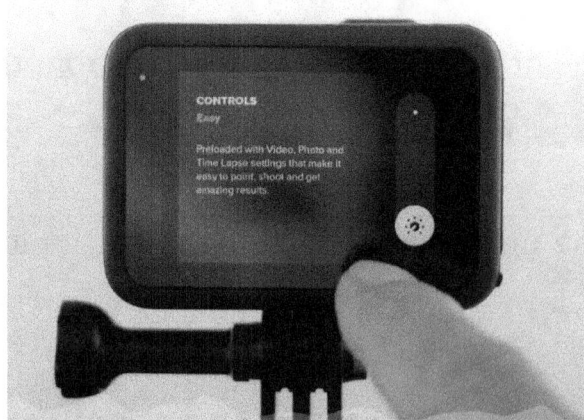

Easy Controls is great for beginners, while Pro Controls offer advanced features for more experienced users.

CHAPTER SEVEN: Pro Control

P ro control is an important aspect of your GoPro camera as it empowers you to customize the GoPro's preset settings and completely take control of the different camera modes, settings, etc.

Video Preset Mode:

The video mode is the default mode when you turn on the GoPro camera, and the video mode consists of the following preset modes;

- Standard preset mode

- Full Frame preset mode

- Activity preset mode

- Cinematic preset mode

- Slo-Mo presets mode.

You can customize any of the following Preset modes and take stunning photographs.

How to Change Video Preset Mode:

The different preset modes are designed for different situations, such as low light, action sports, or vlogging. By choosing the right preset mode, you can ensure that your footage looks its best. Here is how to change the video preset mode:

- The first step is ensuring the GoPro camera is in Pro control mode.

- The next step is to enter the video record mode

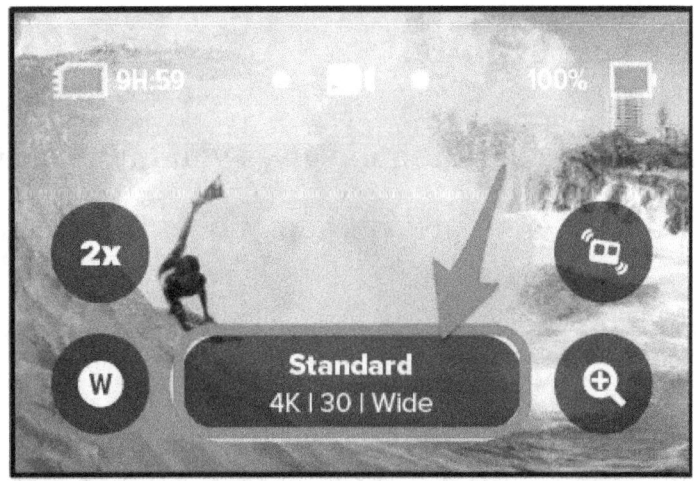

- Ensure to select the preset capture mode.

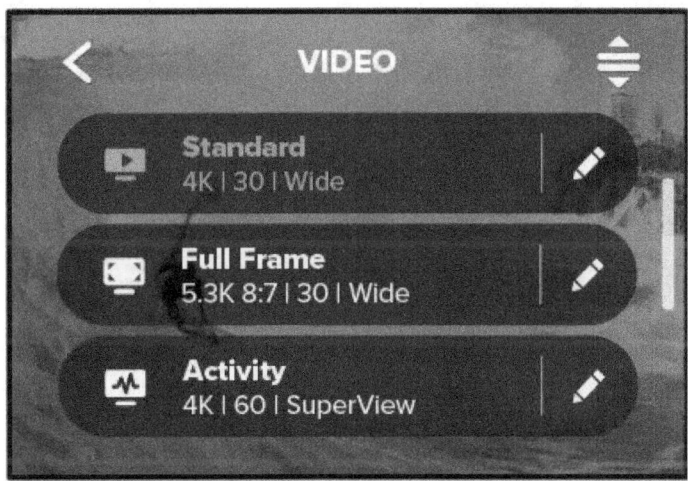

- You will be provided with different preset settings; select the preset you want to use.

Photo Preset Mode:

The Photo Pro control mode gives you total control to select from different preset photo modes such as:

- Photo preset mode

- Burst preset mode

- Night presets mode.

You can also customize any of these modes and create a specific preset photo mode.

Time Lapse

The time-lapse mode has the following preset modes;

- TimeWarp preset

- Star Trails preset

- Light Painting preset

- Vehicle Light Trails preset

- Time Lapse preset

- Night Lapse presets.

You can select any of the following preset modes and customize it.

Customizing The Presets:

To get the best possible image quality for your specific shooting conditions. The default presets are designed for general use, but you can customize them to get the best possible image quality for your specific needs. Here is how to change the preset settings;

- From the capture screen, ensure to select the preset capture mode.

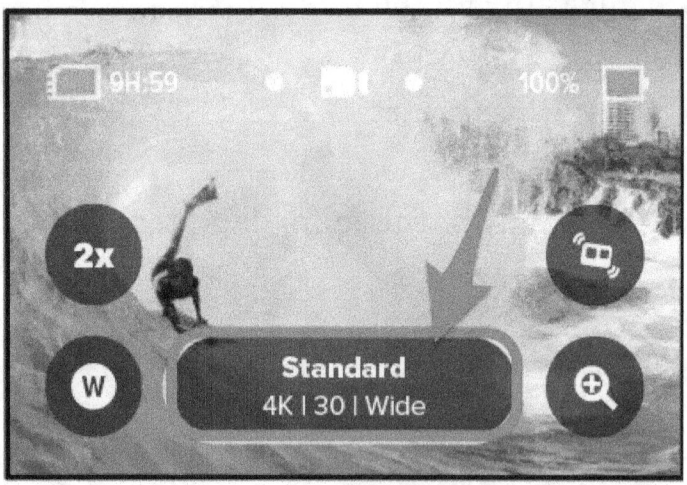

- The next step is selecting the specific preset setting you want to customize.

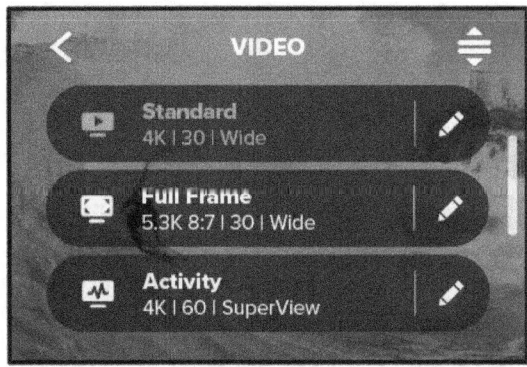

- If this is your first time, you will have an on-screen instruction to guide you on the different settings you can customize.

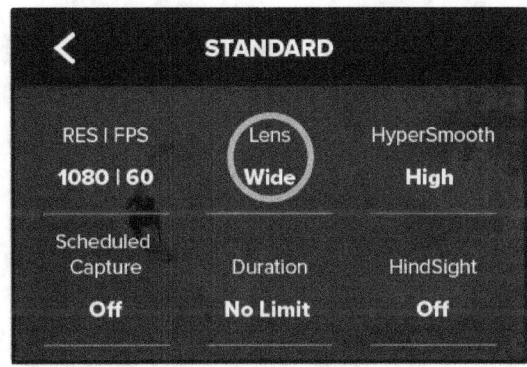

- Tap the back icon to save your changes and return to the presets screen.

Note: You cannot delete the preloaded presets, but you can customize and create your own.

Restoring Customized Preset to their Original Settings:

Suppose you want to go back to your original preset settings; here is how to go about the process:

- From the capture screen, ensure to select the preset capture mode.

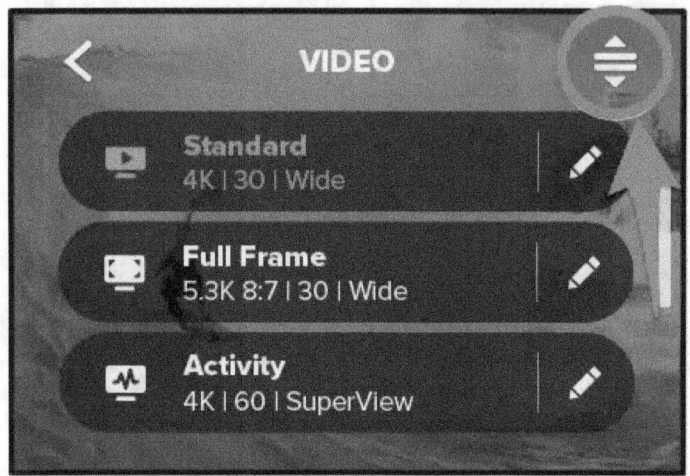

- The next step is to select the **Manage** icon at the top right.

- Proceed to the customized presets you want to restore and tap the restore icon on the side.

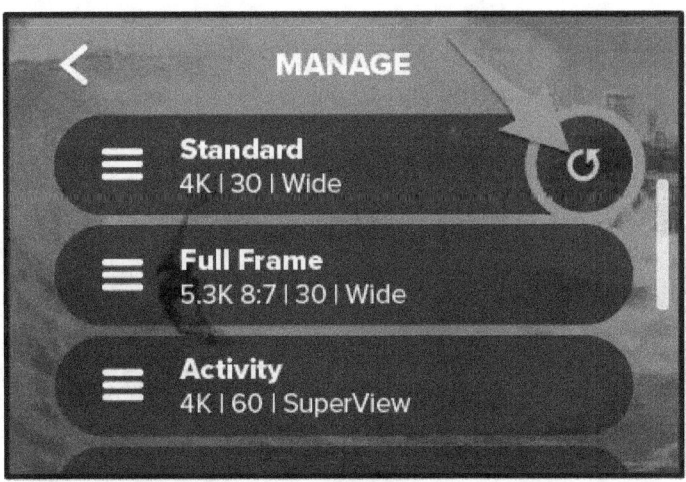

- When you are done, select the back button to save the settings.

This feature is an excellent way of restoring your settings if you accidentally changed the settings of a custom preset or if you need help with what you changed.

How to Create Your Own Presets:

If you frequently shoot in the same conditions, you can create a custom preset with the settings you need to save time. This will save you time from having to adjust the settings every time you start recording. Here is how to create your own preset settings:

- From the capture screen, ensure to select the preset capture mode.

- The next step is to select the **Manage** icon at the top right.

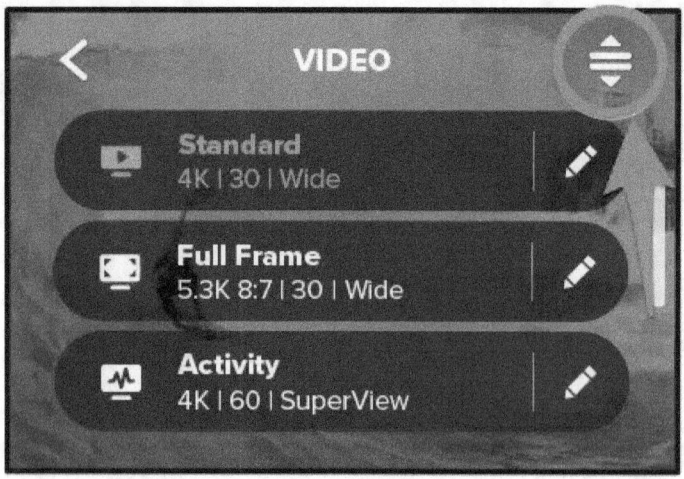

- Tap the plus button in the upper right corner of the camera.

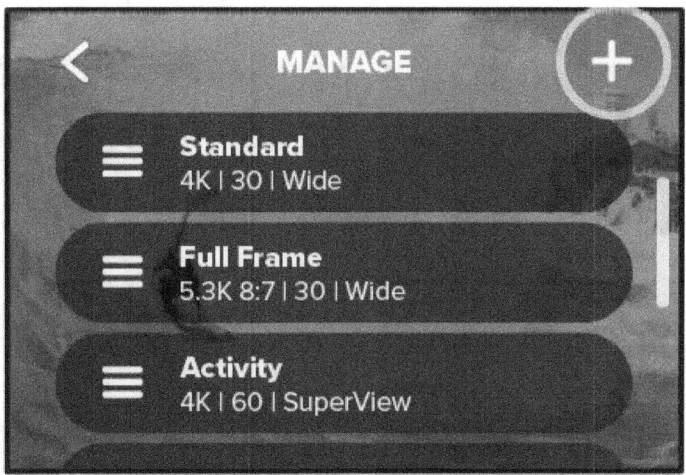

- Ensure to select a specific preset mode that you want to create.

- Follow the on-screen instructions to customize the settings that you want.

- Choose an icon and name for your preset and tap the save icon to save the new presets.

Note: You will see on-screen instructions that will guide you through the options that are customizable.

CHAPTER EIGHT: GoPro Hero Power Tools

GoPro Hero Power Tools are a set of features that help you capture more creative and interesting footage with your GoPro Hero 12. In this chapter, you will learn how to use the power tools.

The power tools consist of the following features:

- HindSight

- Scheduled Capture

- Duration Capture

HindSight:

HindSight continuously records video in the back-ground, ensuring you never miss a moment. This feature lets you capture 30 seconds of video before pressing the shutter button, ensuring you get all the moment, even if you're a bit late to start recording.

How to Set Up HindSight:

HindSight means you'll always take advantage of every moment, even if you're a bit late pressing record. Here is how to set up this feature:

- The first step is to select the video preset you want to record; then, touch and hold the capture settings to reveal the menu.

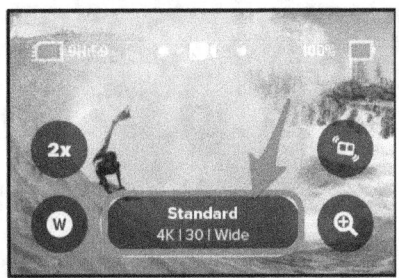

- The next step is to select HindSight from the options.

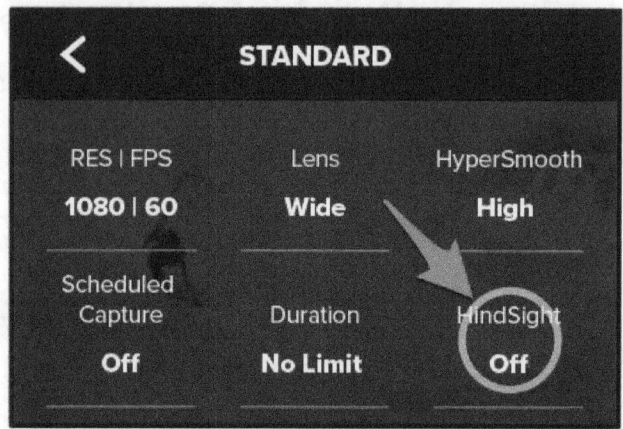

- Here, you can set HindSight for either 15 or 30 seconds.

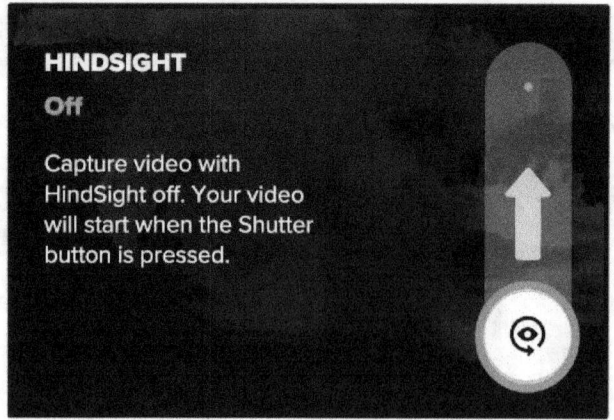

- When HindSight is turned on, you will see the HindSight icon on the rear touch screen.

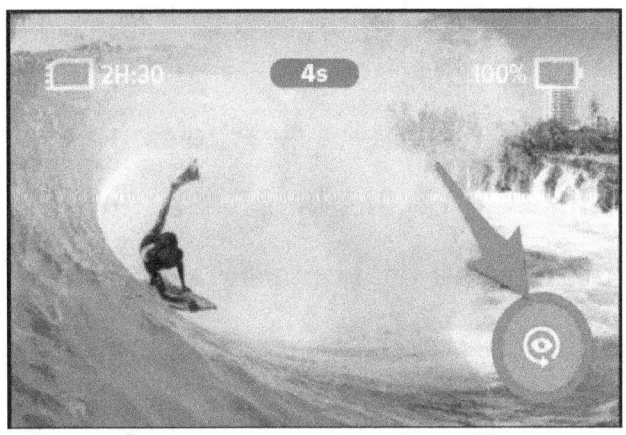

- You can press the Shutter button at any time to start recording.

NOTE: When the HindSight buffer is full, the indicator located at the top center of the screen turns blue. This indicates that your camera has stored the previous 15 or 30 seconds of video. Please note that pressing the Shutter button to start recording will only save the video.

If you want to save battery power, you can tap on the option Stop HindSight anytime to cancel it. Additionally, if you have not started recording 15 minutes after turning on HindSight, your camera will automatically pause it to help conserve battery power.

Scheduled Capture:

Scheduled Capture is a great way to capture something that happens at a specific time, like a sunrise or sunset. This feature lets you set a timer for your camera to start recording. This is useful for capturing things like sunrises or sunsets.

When Scheduled Capture is enabled, you can set the camera to start recording at a specific time and date. This is a great way to ensure that you don't miss a once-in-a-lifetime event.

How to Set Up Scheduled Capture:

Schedule your GoPro to automatically capture a shot up to 24 hours before for all presets. Here is how to set the scheduled capture feature on:

- The first step is to select the video preset you want to record; then, touch and hold the capture settings to reveal the menu.

- The next step is to select Scheduled Capture from the options.

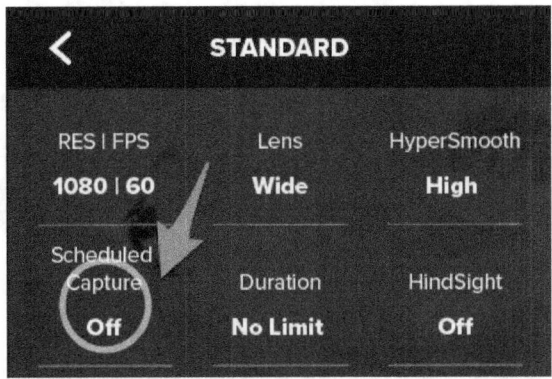

- Here, you can set the time you want your GoPro to capture the shot.

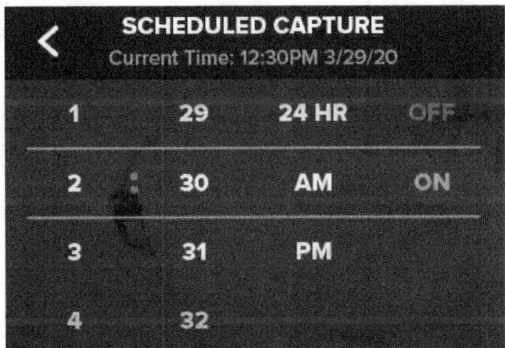

- Once you have set the time, you can either turn off your GoPro or continue using other settings on your camera.

Duration Capture:

This feature lets you limit how long your camera will record. This is useful for preventing your camera from running out of storage space. This feature lets you limit how long your camera will record. This is useful for preventing your camera from running out of storage space.

How to Set Up Duration Capture:

Set the recording duration of your GoPro in Video, Time-Warp, Time Lapse, and Night Lapse modes from 15 seconds to 3 hours. Here is how to set up this feature:

- The first step is to select the video preset you want to record; then, touch and hold the capture settings to reveal the menu.

- The next step is to select the **duration** from the options.

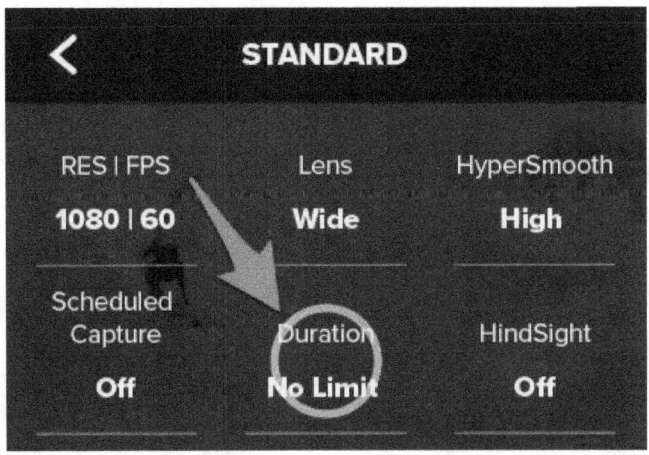

- Here, you can select the duration for your shot.

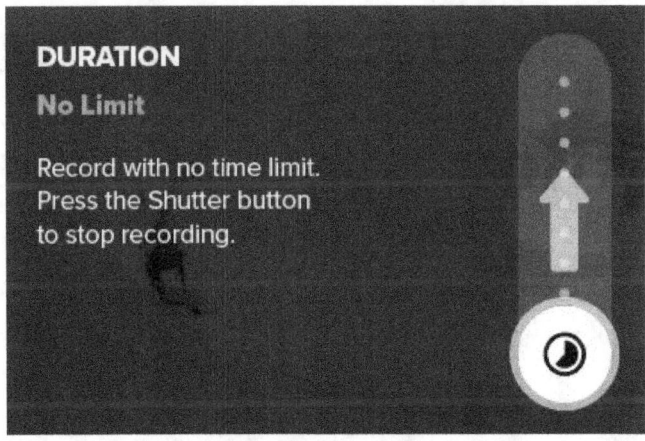

- Start recording by pressing the Shutter button. Your GoPro will automatically stop recording after the set duration.

CHAPTER NINE: GoPro Customization

GoPro customization refers to the ability to change the appearance and functionality of a GoPro camera to suit your individual needs and preferences. In this chapter, you will learn how to customize your GoPro Hero 12.

How to Record with QuickCapture:

QuickCapture is a feature on the GoPro Hero 12 that allows you to start recording video or taking photos with a single button press. This is a great way to capture moments quickly and easily without fumbling with the camera's settings.

- Press the Shutter button to start recording. Press it again to stop recording and turn off your camera.

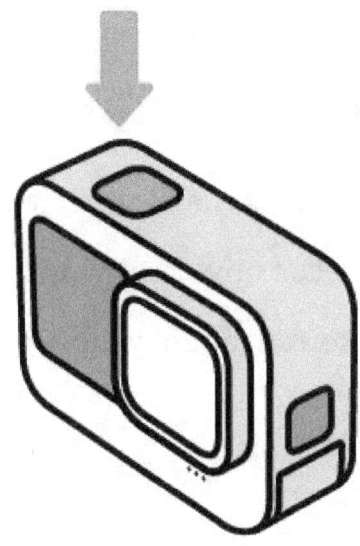

Turn Off QuickCapture: By default, QuikCapture is enabled, but you can turn it off. To access the Dashboard, swipe down on the rear screen and select turn off Quick-Capture.

NOTE: When you use QuikCapture, the camera will automatically begin recording with your most recently used video settings.

Adding HiLight Tags:

HiLight Tags is a feature that allows you to mark specific moments in your video as they happen. This can be useful for identifying moments you want to remember or creating a highlight reel of your footage.

To add a HiLight Tag, press the Mode button on the side of the camera while recording or playing back video. The camera will make a sound, and a yellow dot will appear on the video timeline.

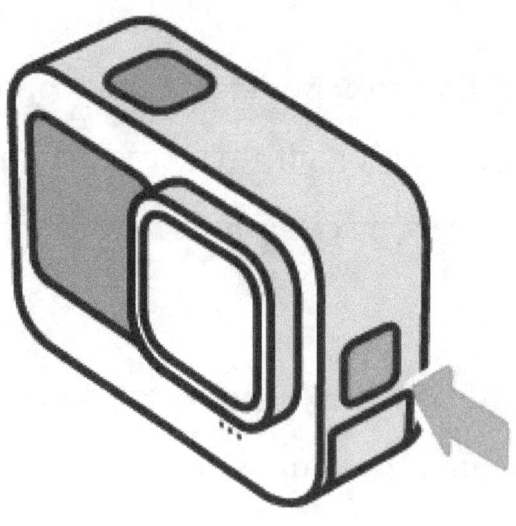

HiLight Tags can be viewed in the Quik app or Quik for Desktop. In the app, tap the **"HiLights"** tab to see a list of all of your tagged videos. In Quik for Desktop, click the **"HiLights"** button in the toolbar.

NOTE: You can remove a HiLight Tag by pressing the Mode button again while recording or playing back video or by pressing the X button in the Quik app or Quik for Desktop.

TIPS: I usually advise GoPro users to use the HiLight Tags for the following reasons: when you are recording a sporting event, vacation, funniest moments, a music video, a vlog, etc.

When recording anything else, you can use HiLight Tags to mark any moment you want to remember or share. Be generous with your tags. Don't be afraid to tag every moment that you think is worth remembering.

GoPro Screen Orientation:

The GoPro has a built-in screen that can be easily rotated to portrait or landscape orientation. When you mount your GoPro upside down, your videos or photos will be recorded or snapped upside down. Here's how to change the screen orientation:

- The first step is to slide down from the top screen of your camera to reveal the **Dashboard**.

- The next step is to swipe left and select the **Preferences** option

- Ensure to select **Displays** and tap **Orientation**.

- Here, you can select either **All** (default) or **Landscape**.

Locking Screen Orientation:

Locking the screen orientation in landscape or portrait orientation is a way to stabilise your footage. This is especially useful when you're using body and handheld mounts. Here's how to use the screen orientation:

- The first step is to swipe down from the top of the GoPro screen to reveal the Dashboard.

- The next step is to position your camera in the orientation you want; then, select the **direction icon** on the Dashboard.

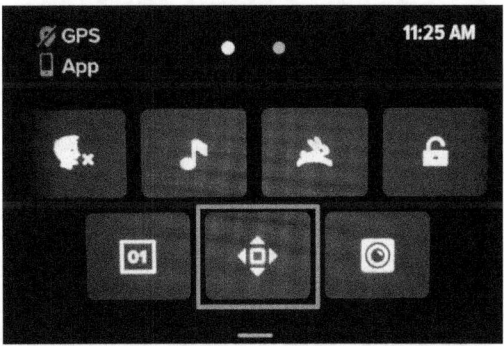

The screen will be locked and will match the orientation of your camera.

CHAPTER TEN: Recording Video

The GoPro Hero has different preloaded video presets when recording or filming. In this chapter, you will learn how to use and manipulate your GoPro Hero 12 video recording.

Standard Recording:

The Standard preset in GoPro Hero 12 is a good all-around setting that is suitable for most situations. It provides a good balance of image quality and stabilization. The Standard preset uses the following settings:

Resolution: 5.3K | **Frame rate:** 30fps | **Digital Lens:** Wide | **HyperSmooth:** On | **Color:** GoPro Color | **White**

Balance: Auto | **ISO:** Auto | **Sharpness:** Medium | **Noise Reduction:** Low

NOTE: A flexible preset is suitable for general recording purposes. It records in 5.3K resolution (1080p when using the Extended Battery setting) at a rate of 30 frames every second for optimal viewing on both mobile devices and television.

The lens is adjusted to a broad setting to encompass a larger portion of the scene. You can adjust these settings to suit your specific needs.

Full Frame:

The Full Frame preset in the GoPro Hero 12 video preset uses an 8:7 aspect ratio. This means that the video will be wider than it is tall, which is ideal for capturing landscapes and other wide-angle shots. The Full Frame preset also uses the Linear field of view, providing the most accurate scene representation.

The Full Frame preset is available in the following video resolutions and frame rates: 5.3K at 60 fps, 4K at 60 fps, 2.7K at 60 fps, or 1080p at 60 fps. You can use the full frame preset for the following purpose: Vlogging, Cycling, Skiing, Snowboarding, etc.

Activity:

The activity mode captures special intense moments and records with 4k at 60 fps with the SuperView digital lens. This recording mode gives your footage a classic video coverage with high-resolution, full-screen playback.

Cinematic Mode:

Experience the magic of high-resolution video with the Cinematic preset. This video mode captures stunning 5.3K video at a smooth 30 frames per second. The Cinematic mode uses a Linear digital lens, which adds effects to boost great cinematic footage.

Slow-Motion:

The Slow-Mo preset is the perfect choice when it's time to capture fast-paced action shots in slow motion. This video mode records an impressive 2.7K resolution at a whopping 240 frames per second using the Wide lens.

This allows you to slow down your footage up to eight times the normal speed during playback, revealing astonishing details that often escape the naked eye.

On-Screen Shortcuts:

Here are some on-screen shortcuts that can be carried out when recording videos with the GoPro camera:

Slo-Mo: Before using the Slow-Mo video recording mode, you can select the recording speed by tapping the Slo-Mo shortcut icon.

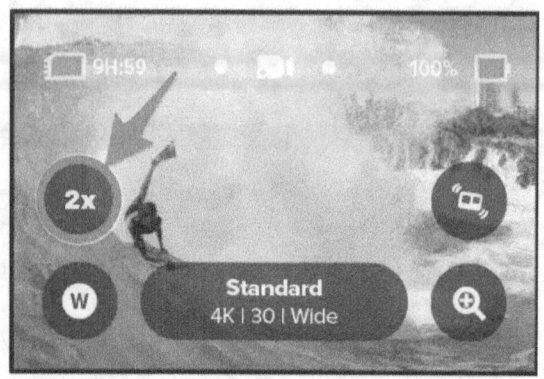

The next step is to use the slider to choose the slow motion that you want to record your video with (e.g., 1x, 2x, 4x, or 8x). After you have selected the specific Slow-Mo, press the Shutter button to start recording.

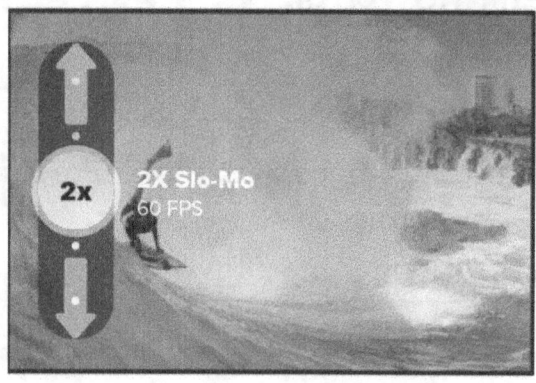

Digital Lenses: Think of changing digital lenses on your GoPro as swapping out lenses on a traditional camera. These lenses impact your shot's appearance, including how much you can see, how close or far things appear, and whether there's a curved effect. Here's how you do it:

- Ensure to tap the digital lens shortcut icon, and you'll see a list of options.

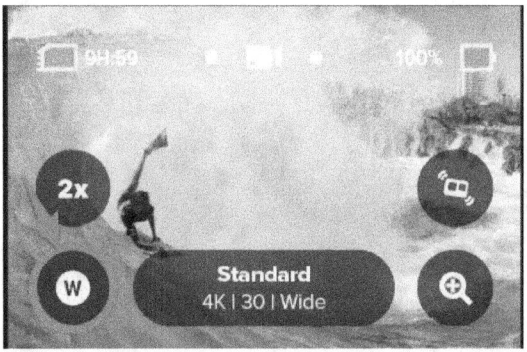

- You can even preview how each option changes your shot in real time.

- Once you find the look you want, just tap it.

- Remember that some of these digital lenses only work with specific frame rates. If that's the case, your GoPro will adjust the frame rate automatically when you switch lenses. So, no need to worry about it.

HyperSmooth: The HyperSmooth is feature that allows you quickly choose your level of video stabilization.

- Tap the hypersmooth shortcut icon before you start recording.

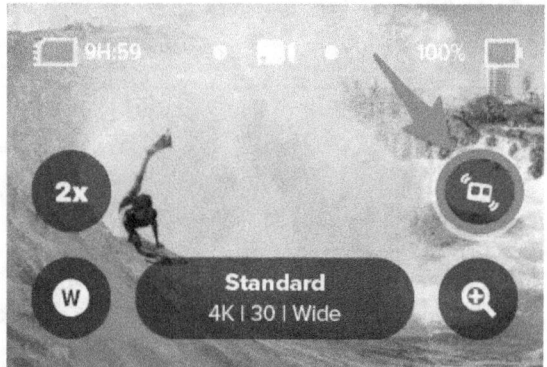

- Then, use the slider to select from the following options: HyperSmooth Off, On, Boost, or Auto-Boost.

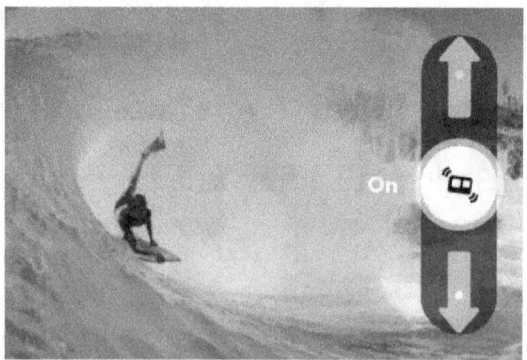

Zoom: You can use the zoom feature to capture your footage in a closer range.

- Ensure to select the zoom icon, then use the zoom slider to adjust (increase or decrease) the zoom level.

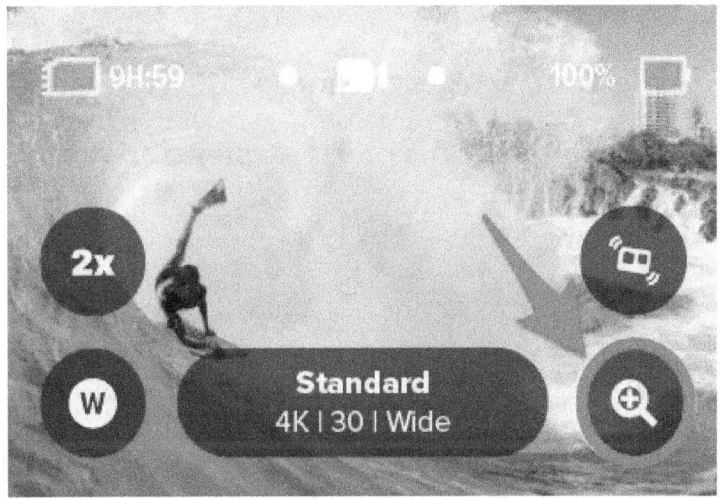

- After you have adjusted the zoom level, the zoom will be locked until you readjust it, switch capture modes, or turn off your camera.

CHAPTER ELEVEN:
Video Settings

I n this section, you get to choose how your videos will look. Don't worry; it's pretty straightforward!

RES | FPS:

Imagine your video as a picture on your TV or computer screen. You can pick how that picture fits on the screen, how clear it is, and how smooth it moves.

Aspect Ratio: Think of this as the shape of your video.

Resolution: This is about how sharp your video looks.

Frame Rate (FPS): This controls how smoothly your video plays. It's like how many pictures are shown every second.

Just tap on the one you like, and your camera will pick your best settings. For example, if you choose the 16:9 shape, your camera will set it to a high-quality video with 60 smooth pictures every second. If you change your mind, tap something else.

Lenses:

This part is about picking the right "digital lens" for your shot. It's like choosing different camera angles. You can choose from the following—HyperView, SuperView, Wide, Linear + Horizon Lock/Leveling, or Linear. The best one depends on the quality and smoothness you want in your video.

Recording Duration/ Interval (Looping):

You can decide how long your camera records before stopping by itself. By default, it's set to 5 minutes, but you can change it if you want.

Video Stabilization (HyperSmooth):

Here's a cool feature! If you're doing action-packed stuff like biking or skiing, HyperSmooth makes your video super steady, almost like using a fancy stand. You can turn it on, boost it, or let it work automatically to keep your video smooth.

Scheduled Capture:

You can set a time for your camera to turn on and start recording. It's like telling it when to get ready for action.

HindSight:

HindSight is like a time machine for your video. You can choose to save the 15 seconds or 30 seconds just before you press the record button. Great for capturing unexpected moments!

Timer:

Need some time to get ready before you start recording? You can set a 3- or 10-second timer to give you a little countdown.

Touch Zoom:

Touch Zoom lets you get closer to the action with a simple touch. Just slide your finger to zoom in or out.

ProTune:

ProTune is for the pros who want to control advanced settings. You can tweak things like Bit Rate, Color, ISO Limit, Exposure, and microphone settings to get your video just right.

That's it! You're all set to capture some amazing moments with your GoPro.

CHAPTER TWELVE:
Taking Photos

Your GoPro camera has three handy photo presets, and it's super easy to use them, even if you're new to this. Just pick the kind of photo you want, and then press the Shutter button to take the shot.

All the photos it takes will be 27 megapixels in size, which is great for sharing on social media. They also have this cool 8:7 aspect ratio that fits well on your feeds.

Photo (DEFAULT):

If you use this preset, your GoPro will work magic with SuperPhoto image processing. When you press the Shutter button once, it captures a single photo.

Burst:

Now, Burst mode is where the action happens. It's like taking a whole bunch of photos really quickly. So, if you're trying to capture fast-moving stuff, like sports or your dog doing zoomies, this is your go-to preset.

Depending on the lighting, it can take up to 30 photos in just one second. That's seriously speedy!

Night:

Finally, we have the Night preset. It's pretty smart because it adjusts your camera's settings to let in more light when it's dark or dim. This is perfect for those low-light situations. But here's the catch – it's not ideal for photos when your camera is moving around a lot.

Note: If you're on the go, stick to the other presets for better results. Just remember to choose the right one for your situation, press that Shutter button, and let the camera do its thing!

On-Screen Shortcuts:

The photo presets feature four default shortcuts, but you can swap them out with any shortcuts you'd like.

Photo Timer: The Photo Timer is a feature that allows you to time the GoPro Hero camera. Here's how to enable this feature; Tap the timer shortcut icon on your camera app. It looks like a clock.

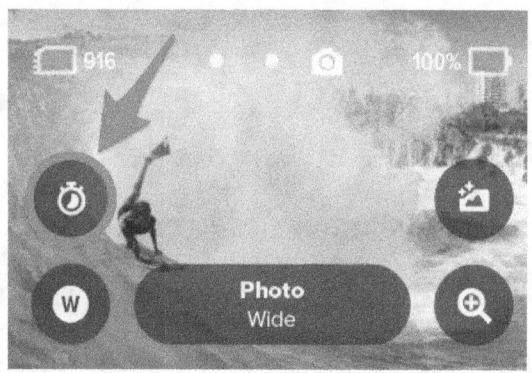

Choose the time count that you want for your photo. Select a 3-second countdown for selfie photos. Select the 10-second countdown for group photographs. Press the Shutter button, and your camera will start the countdown.

Digital Lenses: Digital lenses are like magical filters for your photos. They can change how much you see in your picture, crop the image, or even give it a cool fisheye look. Try switching between these lenses to find the one that makes your shot look the best.

- Tap the digital lenses shortcut icon.

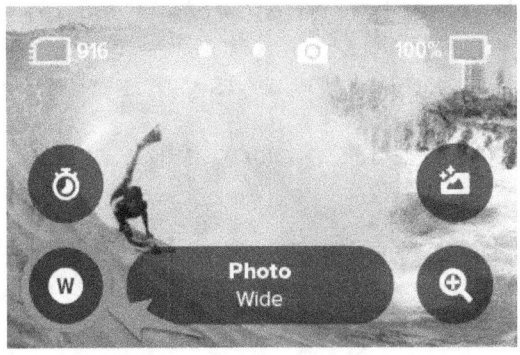

- Scroll through the options to see a live preview of each option, then tap the one you want.

Output: Your GoPro camera lets you choose how it handles and saves your photos. When you use the 'Photo mode,' which means taking one photo at a time, you have more choices and control over the outcome. Select the **output icon** and the options you want to use.

CHAPTER THIRTEEN: Mounting Your GoPro

The GoPro can be mounted in different positions to capture special moments of your actions that are often impossible with traditional cameras.

You can mount the GoPro camera in positions such as on your helmet, chest, bike handlebars, or even a drone to achieve dynamic and immersive shots.

In this chapter, you'll learn how to mount the GoPro Hero 12 camera to capture exciting sporting and outdoor activities where manual operation is challenging. So, let's get started!

Choose Your Mount:

Before starting, deciding where you want to mount your GoPro Hero 12 to capture the moment is important. Here are some of the most common mounting options:

- Helmet mount

- Chest mount

- Handlebar mount (for bikes and motorcycles)

- Tripod or selfie stick mount

- Suction cup mount (for cars and windows)

- Adhesive mount (for flat surfaces)

- Drone mount (if you're using a drone)

The Mounting Hardware:

Below are the items that can be used to mount your Go-Pro Hero 12:

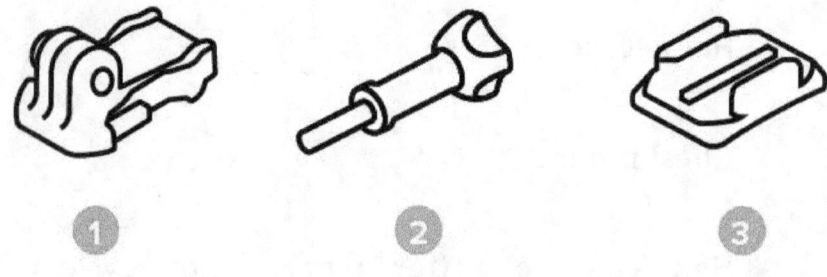

- Mounting Buckle

- Thumb Screw

- Curved Adhesive Mount

Mounting Your GoPro

Using the mounting fingers on your GoPro camera is easy, and it depends on your mount type.

- First, determine the type of mount you're using. There are two options: mounting with a buckle or attaching your GoPro directly to the mount.

- If you are using a buckle, flip the folding fingers on your GoPro camera down into the mounting position. You'll find these folding fingers on the bottom of your camera.

- Now, it's time to connect your camera to the mount. Here's how:

- Interlock the folding fingers on your camera with the mounting fingers on the buckle. They should fit together like puzzle pieces.

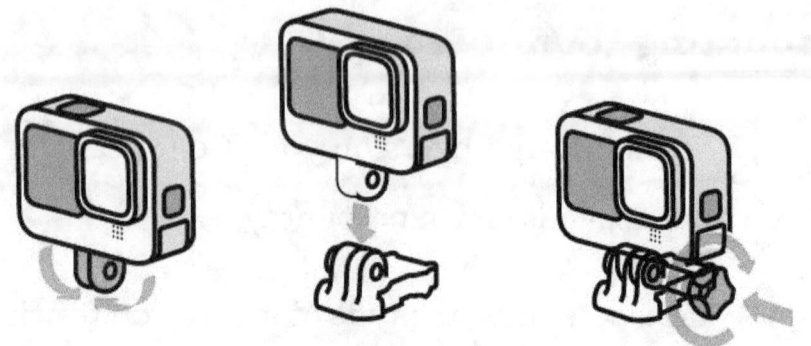

- Once they're aligned, secure your camera to the mounting buckle using a thumb screw. This keeps your camera firmly attached.

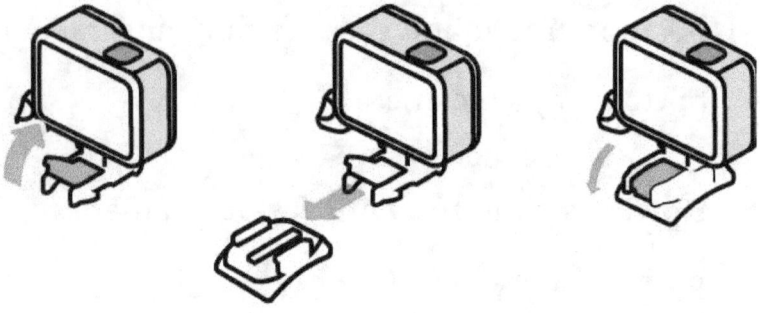

- That's it! You're ready to capture your adventures with your securely mounted GoPro. Enjoy and capture those amazing moments.

Using Adhesive Mounts:

Here is how to use the adhesive mounts on your GoPro Hero 12.

- **Timing is Everything:** Give your mounts some time to get cozy. Attach them at least a day before you plan to use them.

- **Smooth Surfaces are Best:** Adhesive mounts work best on smooth surfaces, not on things like rugged terrain or bumpy textures.

- **Press Like You Mean It:** When you're attaching the mount, give it a good, firm press. Make sure the adhesive is making full contact with the surface.

- **Clean and Dry is Key:** Keep it clean and dry! Before you attach anything, make sure the surface is squeaky clean.

CHAPTER FOURTEEN: GoPro Tips & Tricks

Here are some tips and tricks that can help you explore the GoPro Hero 12 better:

Maintenance Tips for Your GoPro HERO12 Black

Taking care of your GoPro HERO12 Black is essential to ensure it performs at its best. Don't worry; it's easier than it sounds. Here are some simple steps to keep your camera in top shape:

Waterproof Functionality:

- Your GoPro HERO12 Black is waterproof up to 33ft (10m) without the need for additional housing. That means you can use it confidently around water, dirt, or sand.

- Just make sure the camera door is securely closed before diving in.

Check the Seal:

- Before sealing the door, ensure that the rubber seal is clean and free from any debris.

- Use a cloth to wipe it down if necessary.

Keep It Dry and Clean:

- Before opening the camera door, make sure it's dry and free of dirt.

- If your GoPro gets sandy or muddy, give it a gentle rinse with fresh water and dry it off with a cloth.

Dealing with Hardened Debris:

- Sometimes, sand or debris can get stuck around the camera door.

- If that happens, soak your camera in warm tap water for about 15 minutes, then rinse thoroughly to remove any debris. Ensure your camera is completely dry before opening the door.

Audio Maintenance:

- For optimal audio performance, shake your camera or gently blow on the microphone area to remove water and debris.

- Avoid using compressed air as it may harm the camera's waterproof protection.

After Saltwater Adventures:

- If you've been in saltwater, always rinse your camera with fresh water after use.

- Dry it gently with a soft cloth to prevent any salt residue buildup.

Lens Cover Care:

- The lens cover is durable, but it's not indestructible. Keep it clean using a soft, lint-free cloth.

- If any debris gets trapped between the lens and the trim ring, use water or air to flush it out. Never insert foreign objects around the lens.

Taking these simple maintenance steps will help ensure your GoPro HERO12 Black remains in excellent working condition, capturing all your adventures without a hitch. So go ahead, have fun, and capture those amazing moments worry-free!

Turn off GPS & Front Screen:

There's a simple way to make the Hero 12 battery last longer. You can do this by turning off two features: the front screen and the GPS. These are cool features, but they use up a lot of battery.

The front screen is handy when you're shooting a selfie video because it helps you frame yourself correctly. To turn it off, just swipe down from the top of the camera screen and tap the bottom left icon. This will show you the front-screen options.

The GPS is great for tracking things like speed, height, and velocity, which you can then display on your video using the GoPro Player desktop editor. It looks awesome, especially for fast-paced shots like off-road biking. To turn off the GPS, go to your camera preferences and scroll down to the GPS section.

Turn on Pro Controls:

When you're getting started with your Hero 12, it might seem like there's not much you can do. There's a whole world of possibilities waiting for you, and it's called 'Pro Controls.' Don't worry; it's easy to unlock them.

To access all the amazing camera options, follow these simple steps:

1. **Swipe Down:** Start by swiping down from the top of your screen. This action opens up a whole new world of settings.

2. **Swipe Left:** Once you've swiped down, swipe left, and you'll find yourself in the 'Controls' section.

3. **Select Pro Controls:** Now, tap on 'Pro Controls.' That's the key to unleashing the full potential of your Hero 12.

Once you've done this, you'll notice many new options on your video screen. It might seem like a lot at first, but be confident! These options allow you to customize your camera experience like a pro. You can:

- Explore various pre-set video modes.

- Adjust frame rates for that perfect shot.

- Fine-tune the resolution to suit your needs.

- Dive into manual controls with a plethora of settings.

While all these options may seem overwhelming for beginners, it's worth taking the time to experiment and learn what they do. Trust me; you can capture incredible shots and videos by simply playing around with these settings.

Set Bit Rate to High

Now that you've activated the Pro Controls, you can enhance the quality of your videos. One way to do this is by increasing the bit rate. When you increase the bit rate, your Hero 12 camera will capture more details in each video, making it look much better.

This is especially important for recording moving scenes because the more details the camera captures, the smoother your video will appear. Another interesting option is located right next to the Bit Rate setting, and it's called '10Bit Color.'

Turning on this option expands the range of colors in your videos from millions to billions. However, remember that to take full advantage of this feature, you'll need to use video editing software like Premiere Pro, which may only be suitable for some.

NOTE: Be aware that enabling these options will result in larger video file sizes.

Change White Balance to 5500K

White balance is like a magic knob in your camera that controls the colors in your videos. It's measured in Kelvin, and the cool-to-warm spectrum is what you need to know.

- **Cool (Blue)**: If you set it to a lower Kelvin value, your video will have cooler, bluish tones.

- **Warm (Yellow)**: On the other hand, if you go for a higher Kelvin value, your video will look warmer, with yellowish tones.

By default, most cameras, including the Hero 12, are set to 'Auto White Balance.' This means the camera tries to figure out the right white balance as the lighting changes around you.

However, here's the catch: The Hero 12 isn't always great at picking the perfect white balance, which can affect your video quality.

So, here's a tip: You can manually choose a fixed white balance setting for better results.

A good option for most situations is the '5500K' setting. It works well on both cloudy and sunny days and generally gives you the best colors. You might only want to adjust it when you're shooting at night, where a cooler tone could be more suitable.

So, in a nutshell, adjusting your camera's white balance can make a big difference in how your videos look. Remember, it's like a magic color control for your camera, and a little tweak can go a long way!

Choose the Right Field of View + Stabilization Option:

In the previous GoPro camera models, you've had the choice to pick a different field of view settings. The field of view basically determines how wide your shot is and how much of the scene it includes. The Hero 12 offers various options, like Linear and HyperView, each offering a different view.

Now, depending on the type of video you want to create, you'll want to choose the right field of view or "Lens" setting. If you plan to capture intense action with lots of movement, like extreme sports, Linear + Horizon Lock is your best bet. It helps keep your video steady and smooth.

On the other hand, if you want to make things look faster, like in FPV shots or when recording motorbike or car scenes, the HyperView option is excellent. It gives the impression of a much higher speed than reality.

For vlogging purposes, I'd recommend going with the Wide Lens option. This setting allows you to capture more of your surroundings while maintaining a natural look in your videos.

In a nutshell, your choice of field of view or lens setting depends on the type of video you're making, so pick the one that suits your needs best!

Use Voice Commands

The GoPro Hero 12 Black has a cool feature: you can tell it what to do with your voice, so you don't have to touch it. It's like having a little assistant! You can say things like "GoPro, start recording," "GoPro, stop recording," or "GoPro, take a photo." It's pretty handy, but to use it best, make sure you check out all the things you can say to it and talk to it clearly when you do. This way, you'll get the most out of this cool voice control feature!

Take Advantage of QuickCapture

Imagine you're out and about and suddenly see something you want to capture—a hilarious moment or a beautiful view. But here's the catch: your camera is turned off, and you don't have time to fumble with settings. That's where QuickCapture comes to the rescue!

QuickCapture is a nifty feature that lets you start recording a video or take a photo instantly, even if your camera is off. It's super easy to use. Just press the shutter button once, and you'll start recording a video. If you want to snap a quick photo, hold down the shutter button for a few seconds.

This feature is perfect for those spontaneous moments when you need to capture something in the blink of an eye. No more missing out on those memorable shots because your camera isn't ready. With QuickCapture, you're always prepared to seize the moment!

Use the GoPro App

The GoPro app helps you do some pretty cool stuff, like checking out your photos and videos before you take them, tweaking your camera settings, and even doing some quick edits while you're out and about.

Just grab your smartphone and download the app to get in on the action. Then, make sure to connect it to your camera. This way, you'll have everything in sync, making it super easy to handle your camera and all the cool stuff you capture.

About the Author

Praixel Fadal is a celebrated technology author, best known for her ability to simplify complex gadgets for everyday users. Praixel has always been passionate about helping others navigate the constantly evolving world of technology.

With an uncanny knack for understanding the unique challenges faced by beginners, she has dedicated her career to writing comprehensive, accessible guides for a wide range of devices.

Apart from writing, Praixel is a voracious reader herself and an advocate for digital literacy. She believes in the transformative power of reading and the crucial role technology can play in making books accessible to all.

www.ingramcontent.com/pod-product-compliance
Lightning Source LLC
Chambersburg PA
CBHW062324290526
45794CB00005B/1885